ALLEN PHOTOGRAPHIC GUIDES

THE CASPIAN HORSE

CONTENTS

INTRODUCTION

DESCRIPTION AND ORIGIN

The Caspian is an ancient breed of small horse, recently rediscovered in northern Iran, on the southern shores of the Caspian Sea. Although rare, small numbers still exist in a semi-feral state in the rice paddies, cotton fields and forests of the remote Elburz Mountains. Known as Mouleki or Pouseki (little muzzle), they are used mainly by the peasant community as pack or cart animals and for winnowing wheat.

The Caspian has the characteristics of a horse and, in varying degrees, resembles the Anglo-Arab. The smaller specimens stand around 9 hands, the average being 11.2 hands but, with better care and husbandry, a small number have exceeded 13 hands in the United Kingdom.

Between 1965 and 1998 almost 700 pure bred Caspians have been registered in Iran, the United Kingdom, Australia, New Zealand and the United States. Small numbers are also present in Japan, France, Brussels, Norway and Sweden.

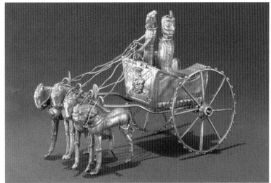

© The British Museum

HISTORY OF THE BREED

Evidence that a horse of Caspian type existed as early as 3,000 BC can be found in the form of ancient writings and artefacts. A terracotta plaque from second millennium BC Mesopotamia, showing a small horse ridden with a nose ring can be seen in the British Museum. During the Mongolian Wars, and again during the Iranian Revolution, much of the documentation relating to the Caspian was destroyed. However, substantial evidence of the history of the Caspian remains.

It is certain that these animals were highly prized for ceremonial purposes as well as for their agility. King Shapur (AD 260) and King Ardashir l (AD 224) were both depicted on stone reliefs with small horses which stood no more than waist high. Horses of Caspian type were presented as gifts to King Darius the Great, which is recorded on the stone staircase of the ancient Palace at Persepolis. The 'gift' horses probably originated from Hamadan, where recent excavations revealed bones thought to be those of the early Caspian horse and other horse breeds, all of which were distinguishable from the bones of the Onager. Artefacts forming part of the Oxus Treasure also depict small horses of similar type. Further proof of the existence of such a horse, and of the esteem in which the Caspian was held, lies in the inclusion of the tiny equid on the cylindrical royal seal of King Darius in 500 BC. A king's fitness to rule was judged by his bravery and prowess at killing lions loosed in his Persian game park, when the acceleration and agility of the horses harnessed to his chariot was crucial.

Of the four horse types, horse type 4, originally thought to be the Arab horse, is now thought to be the Caspian horse of Iran.

Pony Type 1	*Pony Type 2*	*Horse Type 3*	*Horse Type 4*	*Caspian Horse*
Exmoor type not more than 13 hands	Taller and heavier almost Mongolian in type	15 hands – large head and long back	This was previously thought to be the Arab horse	This photograph, taken in Iran, shows the unmistakable likeness of the Caspian to Horse Type 4

'Horse Type 4… with an admixture of Type 3 of Central Asia, is the probable prototype [of the Arabian or oriental horse]. Horse type 4 is certainly recognisable as Arabian and no great stretch of imagination is needed to perceive a possible relationship between the Arab horse and the rediscovered Caspian pony of Iran. It had a high wither, slender legs, a straight or even concave profile, a high carriage of the tail, broad forehead, tapering skull with swelling muzzle and a level croup. We may call it the primeval Arab.'

Elwyn Hartley Edwards
Horses – Their Role in the History of Man (Willow Books, 1987)

REDISCOVERY

For over a thousand years, the Caspian horse of Persia was thought to be extinct until, in 1965, two stallions and a mare were found by Louise Firouz, an American married to an Iranian citizen, who ran a large Equestrian Centre at Norouzabad, just outside Teheran. Between 1965 and 1974, twenty seven foundation animals were

> ### EARLY ANCESTORS
>
> In his research into international horse breeds, Dr Gus Cothran, of Kentucky University, concluded that the Caspian and Turkoman existed at least as early as 3,000 BC and are, almost certainly, ancestral to all forms of the oriental horse.

found, mostly rescued from a life of over-work and disease. Although spirited, they had a kind disposition and were easy to handle. Both mares and stallions were used extensively in the riding school where they excelled at jumping and often competed successfully against much larger horses at local shows. The stallions were ridden by very young children, often in company with mares, and stallions and mares were regularly turned out together.

horse was enforced. Only the stallion, Zeeland, who had been purchased by a New Zealand buyer and refused permission for export, was retained. At the end of the ban, in 1987, Zeeland became the foundation stallion of a new herd in Iran, along with a small number of Caspians found amongst the rehabilitated war horses, following the war with Iraq. During this time they had been used as pack animals and to detonate land mines (fortunately with little success). Louise Firouz also found Alvand, one of the stallions which had been owned by the old Royal Horse Society. At the end of 1998 numbers in

Following the exportation of two mares and a stallion to Bermuda and three shipments to the United Kingdom, between 1971 and 1976, the remainder of the Firouz Caspians were nationalised by the Royal Horse Society of Iran and were auctioned off at the time of the revolution in 1979. All but three were purchased by nomadic tribes, mainly for meat. Due to the scarcity of grain, a ban on keeping more than one

Iran totalled more than sixty. These are owned mainly in two herds: one by The Ministry of Jehad, which has recognised the breed as a national treasure, and the other by John Schneider-Merck, who is attempting to find remnant foundation stock. These are examined thoroughly for type and quality, before being bred on his behalf by Louise Firouz.

DISTRIBUTION AND DEVELOPMENT

IMPORTS TO THE UNITED KINGDOM

In 1971, on the celebration of the Peacock Throne in Iran, a mare and a stallion were given to HRH Prince Philip. During a two-year quarantine in Hungary they produced the filly Atesheh. The mare, Khorshid Kola* and the stallion, Rostam, have had a marked influence on the breed.

Twenty-one Caspians, including in-foal mares, were imported into the United King-

Male foundation lines imported 1971 – 1976	
Ostad*	
Aseman*	
Ruba*	
Felfel*	
Daria Nour*	(imported UK via Bermuda)
Palang*	(imported UK)

*Foundation stock

Ruba*

Ostad* and Aseman*

Palang*

Daria Nour*

dom between 1971 and 1976, mainly by the Caspian Stud UK. These included two mares, a stallion, and their offspring, previously exported by Louise Firouz to Bermuda.

The mare, Hopstone Banafsheh, imported in utero, was the only offspring of the foundation stallion Felfel*.

Female foundation lines imported 1971 – 1976	
Khorshid Kola*	(imported UK)
Pari*	(imported UK)
Shirine*	(imported UK)
Siyah Gosh*	(imported UK)
Mitra*	(imported UK via Bermuda)
Doueez*	(imported UK)
Taloche*	(imported UK)
Fatemeh*	(imported UK)
Alamara*	
Jehan Afrouz*	
Pourandokt*	
Mehri*	
Nour Jehan*	

*Foundation stock

Khorshid Kola*

Shirine*

Siyah Gosh*

Pari*

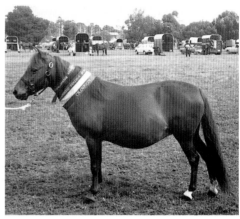

AUSTRALIA AND NEW ZEALAND

Stallions, mares and in-utero foals representing male foundation lines, Daria Nour*, Ruba* and Ostad*, and four female foundation lines, were exported from Iran, via the United Kingdom, to Western Australia in 1975. Seven Caspians, bred mainly by the Caspian Stud UK, were exported in 1978, representing the male foundation lines Aseman* and Palang* and three further female foundation lines. Several of these were subsequently purchased by a stud in New Zealand.

No further exports were made from Iran until 1994, when three second-generation mares, and four stallions, Persicus Kuchek Khan, Persicus Amir, Persicus Yussef and Persicus Nicky, made the hazardous journey through wartorn Azerbaijan, to the United Kingdom. Persicus Tehou and Persicus Amir were sold to Brussels. They represented the following foundation lines:

Male foundation lines exported to the UK in 1994
Secandar Gol*
Zeeland*
Sohrab*

Female foundation lines exported to the UK in 1994
Balsaghar*
Marium Khanum*
Taraneh*
Khorshid*

*Foundation stock

THE UNITED STATES AND SCANDINAVIA

The first four Caspians exported from the United Kingdom to the United States in the 1970s were never bred to pure-bred stock. The first of these was the stallion, Jehan, whose part-bred son still stands in Virginia. Since 1994 a significant number of Caspians has been exported to the United States. These shipments are particularly important as they account for a large proportion of

Caspian youngstock bred in the United Kingdom and Australia since that date. Eight Caspians were exported from the United Kingdom to Norway and Sweden in 1998.

It is also likely that isolated pockets exist elsewhere, since, from the time of Alexander the Great, horses of distinct oriental type have been widely traded via the ancient trade routes.

THE BREED STANDARD

General The Caspian is a horse, not a pony, and therefore should be viewed in the same manner as when judging a Thoroughbred, i.e. the limbs, body and head should all be in proportion to each other. Foreshortened limbs or a head out of proportion are faults. The overall impression should be of a well-bred, elegant horse in miniature.

Eyes Almond shaped, large, dark, set low, often prominent.

Nostrils Large, low set, finely chiselled, capable of considerable dilation during action.

Ears Short, wide apart, alert, finely drawn, often noticeably in-pricked at the tips.

Head Wide, vaulted forehead (in most cases the parietal bones do not form a crest but remain open to the occipital crest). Frontal bone should blend into nasal bone

The typical Caspian head is short and fine with large eyes, set wide apart. The nostrils are large and the ears small and usually markedly in-pricked.

in a pleasing slope. Very deep, prominent cheekbones and great width between cheekbones where they join at the throat. Head tapers to a fine, firm muzzle.

Neck Long, supple neck with a finely modelled throatlatch.

Shoulders and withers Long, sloping, well modelled, with good withers.

Body Characteristically slim with deep girth. Chest width in proportion to width of body. It is a fault to have 'both legs out of the same hole'. Close-coupled, with well-defined hindquarters and good 'saddle space'.

Quarters Long and sloping from hip to point of buttocks. Great length from stifle to hock.

Hocks Owing to their mountain origin, Caspians may have more angled hocks than lowland breeds.

Limbs Characteristically slender with dense, flat bone and flat knees. Good slope to pasterns, neither upright nor oversloping.

Hoofs Both front and back are oval and neat, with immensely strong wall and sole, and very little frog.

Coat, skin and hair Skin thin, fine and supple, dark except under white markings. Coat silky and flat, often with iridescent sheen in summer. Thick winter coat. Mane and tail abundant but fine and silky. Mane usually lies flat (as in Thoroughbreds) but can grow to great lengths. Tail carried gaily in action. Limbs generally clean with little or no feathering at the fetlock.

Colours All colours, except piebald or skewbald (pinto). Greys will go through many shades of roan before fading to near white at maturity.

Height Varies with feeding, care and climate. Recorded specimens have ranged from under 10 hands to over 13 hands. Growth rate in the young is extremely rapid with the young Caspian making most of its height in the first 18 months, filling out with maturity. The average height is 11.2 hands.

Action/performance Natural floating action at all gaits. Long, low swinging trot with spectacular use of the shoulder. Smooth, rocking canter, rapid flat gallop. Naturally light and agile with exceptional jumping ability.

Temperament Highly intelligent and alert, but very kind and willing.

PERFECT CONFORMATION

The Caspian should resemble a well-proportioned miniature horse. Without the inclusion of a person to add perspective, a photograph of a Caspian can give the illusion of a Thoroughbred, Anglo-Arab or Arab horse of 14.2 hands or more. Although of narrow build, few Caspians bred outside Iran have the same 'lean' shape as their Iranian cousins.

The nasal bone is slightly concave, though descendants of the stallion Palang sometimes have a slightly straighter nasal bone, which should still show quality. The domed shape of the forehead which is so prominent in the foals is rarely pronounced in the adult horse.

There is sometimes a strengthening of the muscle under the neck, similar to that of the procession horses at Persepolis, although when the head is held in a 'riding' position, this muscle is rarely in evidence. No doubt this strength was an asset to the carriage horses of Darius.

The mane and tail should be fine and silky and the tail is carried high. Those of stallions, in particular, can be quite abundant.

The summer coat often displays an iridescent sheen.

Bay, chestnut and grey are the most common colours; the greys, and sometimes the bays, changing through roan to white. Occasionally, Caspians born grey change to bay.

Black and dun are less prevalent. Bays and greys, as well as duns, often display the dorsal stripe, shoulder and leg stripes, which are indicative of primitive species.

THE CASPIAN AND OTHER BREEDS

Louise Firouz recorded several marked differences between the Caspian horse and other breeds.

- There is a bulging of the parietal bones resulting in a pronounced elevation of the forehead and a marked difference in the length of the parietal bones forming the roof of the head, which continue to the back of the skull instead of stopping short of the poll. The inter-parietal bone continues unbroken to the poll. There is no parietal crest.

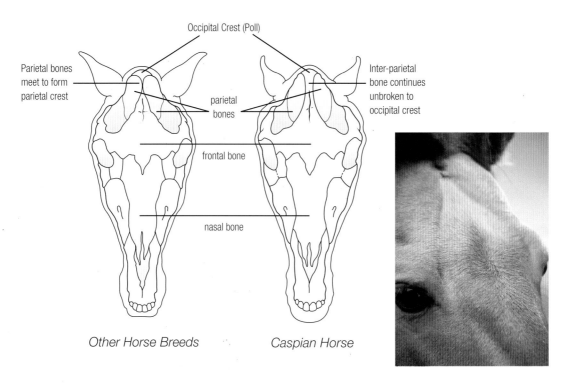

Occipital Crest (Poll)

Parietal bones meet to form parietal crest

Inter-parietal bone continues unbroken to occipital crest

parietal bones

frontal bone

nasal bone

Other Horse Breeds   *Caspian Horse*

This formation of the frontal and parietal bones forms a shield known as the 'jibbah'. a development of the forehead similar to the Arab horse, which, according to Louise Firouz, indicates that the ancient Caspian is the remnant wild stock from which the Arab was bred.

- An extra molar exists in the place where 'wolf' teeth might appear in other breeds. This is usually shed at two years with the milk teeth.

- The shoulder blade is narrower at the top and wider at the base.

- The cannon bones are longer and slimmer.
- The first six vertebrae are longer than usual, giving the appearance of higher withers and a flatter back.
- The hoof is narrow and oval and rarely needs shoeing. Front and hind hoofs are similar in shape.
- The frog is less pronounced in the Caspian than in other horse breeds.
- Tests carried out at Liverpool University showed marked differences in haemoglobin.

Since their introduction to western management, some of these differences, particularly in the feet, are less marked. The frog is more pronounced and the shape of the front feet is now slightly more rounded than that of Iranian bred Caspians. United Kingdom owners find that Caspians which are ridden or driven extensively need to be shod.

TEMPERAMENT

Caspians are intelligent, bold and curious, yet docile, demonstrating a great love of people. They are extraordinarily friendly, actively seeking eye contact, and

often attach themselves in a dog-like fashion to one person. They have a forgiving nature and rarely show any resentment towards mistakes on the part of the owner. Ridden, they are fast, but manageable, quick to learn and easily trained. They are extremely responsive to the voice.

Caspian stallions are ideal for the first-time stallion owner and are often stabled next to mares without any problems. Stallions have been used as mounts for Riding for the Disabled and at Pony Club events. Breeding mares and stallions are often brought back into work after a long break with a minimum of retraining.

HOT-BLOOD HANDLING

Despite the biddable temperament of the breed, it should be remembered that the Caspian is a hot blood and the management of youngsters by children should be overseen by a knowledgeable person.

BREEDING

With only six sire lines available to breeders between 1971 and 1995, foundation females were of equal importance and a carefully planned programme of cyclic crossing and line breeding was established in the United Kingdom to ensure the retention of as wide a genetic base as possible. Female lines were therefore crossed with each sire line in turn.

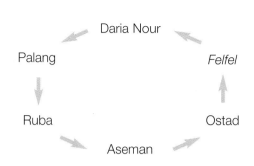

Daria Nour → Felfel

Palang

Ruba ← → Ostad

Aseman

Daria Nour* was noted for jumping, small size, good head and forequarters.
Palang* had good overall conformation but a longer head. He was also taller than average.
Ruba* threw exceptionally good all-round stock, of the smaller type, with a quality head and good temperament.

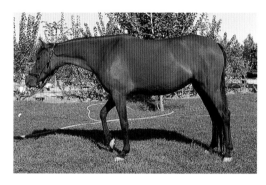

RUBA'S SON

A son of Ruba* (Ruba II) was Supreme Champion at the Salon du Cheval in Paris and a stallion from this line won the 1997 Progeny Award for Hunter Pony Breeding in New Zealand.

Aseman* usually produced stock of the stronger type.
Ostad* was of generally good type and is noted for jumping. This line is represented mainly by the mare Taliyeh, who bred seven stallions.

Felfel* blood line is available only through the 'in-utero' mare Hopstone Banafsheh (out of Taliyeh), who breeds consistently good foals. Stallions from Banafsheh only became available in 1998.

From these emerged three distinct types: a small dainty animal from around 9 hands to 10.1 hands, a slightly taller animal around 11.2 hands, and a larger, stronger animal standing over 12 hands. The original Caspian was probably no more than 9 hands high. Although the occasional 9 hands Caspian still remains, in the United Kingdom height has

increased slightly, with some Caspians reaching over 13 hands. This increase cannot simply be explained by better husbandry or feeding, since animals with the same parentage and under the same management can produce extremes in size. The full sisters, shown here, have a six inch height difference.

In Iran, stock from a large breed will occasionally produce a foal of Caspian size and type. Whilst every effort is made to try to maintain the smaller size it is still too early in the breeding programme to risk narrowing the genetic base by setting preferences for a particular type and most breeders have been careful to ignore personal preferences in order to avoid in-breeding. Consequently, less desirable genes have been maintained along with the more desirable ones. Only when each line is safely established can cautious action be taken in order to alleviate any flaws perpetuated in this way.

The mare, Taliyeh (Ostad line), and the stallion, Forstals Barewa (Daria Nour line), have had the largest impact on the breed. Khorshid Kola* and Ruba* are also well represented. The lines least represented are the female lines, Taloche*, Shirine* and Fatemeh*. The mare Touran, sparsely represented in the United Kingdom, is well represented in Australia and her line is being reintegrated with United Kingdom stock in the United States.

EFFECTS ON OTHER BREEDS

If extensive research, culminating with that of Gus Cothran at Kentucky University, is accepted, then it is likely that the descendants of the Caspian include the Arab, therefore influencing, in varying degrees, many of our modern horse and pony breeds. In a report on his ongoing project to determine the ancestral role of a large number of horse breeds, Cothran states:

Moroccan Barb
Arabian
Persian Arabian
Shagya Arabian
Bedouin Arab
Kurd
Akhal Teke
Yabou
Caspian (Iran)
Caspian (England)

'…the genetic evidence is consistent with the Caspian horse as being ancestral to modern Oriental horses.

'The Caspian is the base breed in a subcluster that also includes the Yabou (a native Iranian breed from the same general area as that where the Caspian was found) and the Turkoman (closely related to the Akhal-Teke). This group represents the most primitive (ancestral) breeds of the Oriental cluster and the Caspian has the most primitive position of these three breeds.'

However, in conclusion, Cothran says: 'this evidence cannot be considered to be proof that the Caspian is the ancestor to modern Arabian type breeds'.

'Regardless of the outcome of future research, the Caspian is a unique breed of horse that deserves the efforts directed at its preservation.'

Gus Cothran

CROSS BREEDING

In the United Kingdom the Caspian has been crossed with the Shetland, Welsh, Dartmoor and Arab. The half-breds shown here are all successful ride and drive animals.

In New Zealand, Caspian stallions have been crossed with either Arab or Thoroughbred mares, then the daughters of such matings have been outcrossed with Thoroughbreds or Arabs. The results, both half- and quarter-breds, are exceptional in looks and performance.

CARE

FEED

A well-fed youngster will attain most of its height in the first 18 months. Care should be taken not to overfeed and it should be remembered that the Caspian is an oriental breed which should be narrow, resembling a riding pony rather than a native breed in body weight. Most Caspians

are good doers and it is advisable not to feed oats or other heating foods, especially if they are to be ridden by children. Alfalfa, sugar beet, chop, carrots, non-heating stable mix and hay are all suitable foods for Caspians, according to the work they are doing. It is advisable to include mineral supplements for breeding mares. As in any breed there are poor 'doers' and adjustments should be made for the individual.

KEEPING AT GRASS/STABLED

Originating in the mountains, the Caspian can be almost deer-like at scrambling over rough ground and browsing available shrubbery. It is not advisable to turn them out on lush pasture because of the risk of laminitis. Whilst they prefer to be turned out, most enjoy being stabled at night. Stable doors should be kept at a suitable height for the small occupants to see over comfortably, whilst remembering that most Caspians are capable of clearing a stable door from a standstill.

WINTERING OUT

The coat of the Iranian Caspian is dense, to protect against the bitter cold of Iranian winters, with a velvet texture. Most Caspians are able to weather extreme cold and can winter out, with adequate shelter and supplementary feed, however, not all Caspians grow the thick coat of the Iranian Caspian. Caspians do not do well in wet conditions; they should be checked regularly in wet weather, and finer-coated animals will probably need the protection of a New Zealand rug. A thick, coarse coat indicates a possible lack of condition.

PROBLEMS

The Caspian is prone to laminitis and sweet itch in the same proportions as other breeds of similar height.

Being a narrow breed, 'sprung' ribs can be quite noticeable in brood mares (they make room for the foal) and note should be taken of all-round condition rather than attempting to cover ribs 'sprung' due to breeding as this could result in overfeeding.

Tooth bumps sometimes appear in youngstock between two and four years old, but these usually disappear quite quickly. In some older animals, pockets of food can become trapped behind the teeth. These should be removed regularly as they can cause ulceration if ignored.

PERFORMANCE

They also compete in dressage and mounted games as well as all the usual ridden and in-hand showing classes. The long smooth stride gives a rider the feel of riding a much larger animal and the sitting trot is extraordinarily comfortable. The length of stride is surprising, in view of the mountain origins of the Caspian, which may account for their exceptional jumping ability and surefootedness. The Caspian is usually a very active little horse and is happier working.

GENERAL

Caspians are extremely versatile and can be used by any member of the family. Most Caspians are perfectly capable of carrying a small adult. They are capable of keeping up with much larger horses at most gaits and are therefore particularly good as lead-rein animals.

Despite their delicate appearance, Caspians are useful working animals which excel at jumping and are regularly used for cross country and as working hunters.

DRIVING

Caspians make exceptional harness horses, combining elegance and agility. As well as single and pair driving, competition successes include *concours d'elegance*, tandem, scurry driving and combined driving. Stallions are regularly ridden and driven, alongside stud duties.

SHOWING

Caspians are successful in lead-rein, first-ridden, ridden-showing, working-hunter

and in-hand classes, occasionally qualifying for Ponies UK. Because of their mountain origins, some Riding Clubs will accept them in Mountain and Moorland classes.

BUYING

POINTS TO LOOK FOR

A 'willowy' appearance is quite normal and does not necessarily indicate that the animal is underfed or malnourished. However, the size should be proportionate and they should not be so narrow that there is no width between the forelegs. Similarly, a Caspian should not have been underfed in order to keep it narrow. Colts have to undergo a stringent veterinary examination in order to obtain a Stallion Licence, therefore, when buying for breeding, colts with parrot mouth, suspect limbs or undescended testicles should be rejected. Care should be taken to try to include rarer bloodlines in breeding plans and some research should be undertaken into the lines available in order to complement the mare or stallion being considered, and to avoid inbreeding.

For showing, particularly lead-rein and first-ridden, a strong underneck muscle should be avoided, though this can usually be improved with correct riding. Particular attention should be paid to hocks, which can be a weak point. A close-coupled body and free gaits are common to most Caspians.

ACKNOWLEDGEMENTS

I would like to thank my family for their support and members of the various Caspian Societies for photographs, help and encouragement throughout. I would also like to thank Louise Firouz for information and photographs; Lez Harvey for line drawings and Gus Cothran for allowing me to use the results of his research. My thanks also to Dru Harper, Mike Burr, Barbara Thomson, Pat McVeagh, Chris Shortis, Jim Moore, and Stine (USA) for additional photographs.

Front cover photograph: the mare Achnaha Klio

British Library Cataloguing-in-Publication Data.
A catalogue record for this book is available from the British Library

ISBN 0.85131.797.9

Published in Great Britain in 2000 by
J. A. Allen an imprint of Robert Hale Ltd.,
Clerkenwell House, 45–47 Clerkenwell Green,
London EC1R 0HT

Series design by Paul Saunders, layout by Dick Vine
Series editor Jane Lake
Colour processing by Tenon & Polert Colour Scanning Ltd., Hong Kong
Printed in Hong Kong by Dah Hua International Printing Press Co. Ltd.